A Fragmented Moment

A Poetic Gathering of the Mind

Hannah Spargo

BookLeaf Publishing

India | USA | UK

Copyright © Hannah Spargo
All Rights Reserved.

This book has been self-published with all reasonable efforts taken to make the material error-free by the author. No part of this book shall be used, reproduced in any manner whatsoever without written permission from the author, except in the case of brief quotations embodied in critical articles and reviews.

The Author of this book is solely responsible and liable for its content including but not limited to the views, representations, descriptions, statements, information, opinions, and references ["Content"]. The Content of this book shall not constitute or be construed or deemed to reflect the opinion or expression of the Publisher or Editor. Neither the Publisher nor Editor endorse or approve the Content of this book or guarantee the reliability, accuracy, or completeness of the Content published herein and do not make any representations or warranties of any kind, express or implied, including but not limited to the implied warranties of merchantability, fitness for a particular purpose.

The Publisher and Editor shall not be liable whatsoever...

Made with ❤ on the BookLeaf Publishing Platform
www.bookleafpub.in
www.bookleafpub.com

Dedication

This goes out to every wandering heart, soul, and mind.

Preface

A collection of poems inspired by the fragmented moments that appear within life.

Acknowledgements

Thank you to every single person who has always helped cultivate my creativity, and lended their support my way.

Wishing You Next to Me

Blissful words and wandering fill my mind,
in the tall sharp grass pricking my thighs.
Sun soaked skin as the reptile next to me.
Watching the damselfly float in its ecstasy.
A young pit bull strong and stoic.
Autumn leaves in the trees as they know it.
A warm kiss from space to earth,
with a crisp nibble of air at its birth.
Blue is the sky, and pink is my heart,
for all the love I feel even tho apart.
I close my eyes and hear your voice
as if you're here despite their choice.
A classic tale reimagined.
A love so strong none could have fathomed.
Being kind to every kind;
with blissful words and a wandering mind.

Rainbows and Daggers

Opalescent hue with summers snow.
Chlorophyll dreams listen to the crow.
Callused hands with a tender heart.
Worries flown high turned into art.
Love like fire.
Dancing with desire.
Impossible becomes possible with you;
giving me hope by cutting the rope,
left dangling as a masked reminder.
This to shall pass as the world takes its flask.
Cheering a toast to the unknown tomorrow;
not knowing if it will bring more sorrow.
Rainbows in rain cutting through clouds with the dagger
of a silver lining;
looking over the fog for the new horizon.

Natures Song

The sun started melting off the trees,
as the shadows started dancing around its' leaves.
Yes, it's true.
Wether light or dark; it's how I feel about you.

Harmony.
True love at its finest.
Balance and empathy.
Nature shows it best.
Just listen close; breathe, and feel the rest.
Harmony.
Harmony.

Water in a wasteland moving freely.
Cotten Candy wonders glowing above me.
Even with the light pollution, I can see you shine.
Along every eternal moment humming you're mine.

Starlit Sonnet

Across a sea of endless motion;
I learned with you how to be open.
A faint flowered breeze kisses my hair,
as I close my eyes just longing to be there.
The sun starts to set, and I feel a golden mellow.
My dreaming becomes dances as I wait for your hello.
The sound a starlit sonnet that will never leave.
My heart is yours forever; it's always you and me.

Heavy Stones

Rain falls like the tears in my eyes.
Time stands still when you're stuck inside.
Moments and memories all fade to grey;
with every locked in space, my soul passes away.
One stone.
Two stone.
Three stone's the charm,
of every harsh thrown word
that causes unseen harm.

Cracked Screen Romance

Reflections in the glasses.
Broken bottles in the way.
I don't even know how we got here today; treading on
the coals as the fire burns my soul
reminiscing of when it all began.

Trials and terrors.
Terrors and trials.
Haunted voices fill our minds.
Demons coming after us.
That's how you know that this is more than lust.
A sacrificial love that won't let go.
Tip toeing in the dark maybe one day I'll know;
the touch of your hand brushing against mine.
Patiently waiting till we're more than fine.

Fractured screens and hearsay lies.
Trust each other before we die.
Held at gun point our hands tied.
Silenced freedom and a locked up cry.

The Dream of Tomorrow

A year is forever.
3 hundred 65 days.
No good mornings.
No good nights.
How am I supposed to survive this life?
Red coated contracts
3 ply deep across my face.
One down.
How many more to go?
Protection and causality
stuck side by side;
pricked for a better future
but no end in sight.
For safety I stand.
A philosophical requiem?
Shouting down with the man.
The American dream.

What Happened

Love can be a nuisance even if it's platonically made.
It's like blue skies and lightning.
You wonder where that could have came.
Grass through the cracks in our cement walls;
broke through every boundary,
now I watch as it all falls.
What happened to trust, and unconditional love...
to sunrise...
late night rides...
conversations in the dark looking through glass above...?
What happened to standing by my side along with the
love of my life?
Torn away.
Gone in the night.
Left with out a trace;
not a glimpse in sight.
A burning girl torn asunder.
Watching the space she's in become silent and crumble.

Dice of Foolery

Fool me once shame on you.
Fool me twice shame on me.
Fool me thrice do I roll the dice?

Prince Cape Daisy

Color me sweet in petals of white.
Radiating color all day and night.
Slow and steady;
wins the race.
Breath shifting hard and fast;
changes the pace.
Cold breeze rocking back and forth.
Kisses of beauty reign on me from the north.
A gentle hand used to pluck;
found now in comfort not in luck.
My stem no longer left intact.
A heart felt moment now a life pact.

Searching Meadows

Lost in Thought.
Crying in the shadows.
We were caught.
Loving in the meadows.
How can it all come crashing down to this?
Why must we end it all because of this?

I've lost you.
I've never felt so far.
I've lost you.
Please tell me where you are?
I'm running and searching.
Clawing and grasping,
just for air.
Hoping to find you, but you're just not there.

The Color of You

Your green eyes, and pink skies.
The color of you.
Your blue home, and gold soul.
The color of you.

I've been everywhere and nowhere.
Stuck in the pocket of my lover.
Reaching out to the skies.
Hopelessly falling to my demise.
Catch me when you can.
I'll be here bathing in
the color of you.

I try to reach you with my hand,
but all I'm grasping is the sand
as I write our names in hearts;
because we're miles and miles apart.

Hypnotized by your guise,
but it's your mind that's the real prize.

Eternal Flower

Soft as the petal.
Strong as the thorn.
Love will live on evermore.

Once Upon a Friend

A moment of peace in a moment of sorrow.
Things may be gone, but bright is tomorrow
for the old has passed,
and a new birthed at last.
There is Freedom in the pain,
and growth from the rain.
A truth can not be silenced,
even when met with quiet violence.
A new light brought forth the dark.
A beautiful journey now to embark.

Distance

Temptations and salutations.
Hierarchies and complications,
but even tho the world around fights tooth and nail;
worse than they ever did in Juliet and Romeos tale.

I have you and you have me.
Even apart, you fulfill my wildest fantasies.
Dreams and songs a mile long.
Longing to caress your skin; I'm here on my knees.

They can keep us apart, but they can't change the state
of my heart.

Cheery Disposition

*How much more hurt can a happy face take before it
breaks?
How many more tears can a happy face yield before it
drops its shield?
How much more can a happy face hide how it really
feels trapped on the inside?
Do you know?
Do you care?
A happy face is in a happy place right?*

My Radiant Pastel

You're a pastel day dream;
yet radiant in everything you sing.

More than Love

How can I say I love you?
I love you just isn't enough.
I need words stronger; than this brew,
in my hands, in this cup.
A burning flame in blue bird radiance;
licking the air craving its oxygen.
A souls true cry not needing an audience.
A biblical passage holding more within.
A love so strong it has no end.
So again, how can I just say I love you...
when your love is forever my mend.

The Path Least Followed

A misty hue that feels taboo in a society of black and grey.
A tingling of color spreads across my skin as I fail to adhere and obey.
This stand still moment is filled with pondering.
My free will soul begins singing with longing.
Follow the masses they scream from their void.
I'm no longer left blind, but instead over joyed.

A Tearful Quill

I'm trying to find the words to say;
as these tears are streaming down my face.
Passages in every tear,
with every memory I held so dear.
The quill marks left on history's page of a relationship
full of yesterday's; has left me feeling how?
They're the only sentence to be formed
right now.

Easy on Yourself

I was wondering what type of grace it is that you were
sold,
because the grace I know will make you whole.

www.ingramcontent.com/pod-product-compliance
Lightning Source LLC
Chambersburg PA
CBHW051135160726
47997CB00019B/2557